Original title:
The Infinite Loop of Life's Questions

Copyright © 2025 Creative Arts Management OÜ
All rights reserved.

Author: Adeline Fairfax
ISBN HARDBACK: 978-1-80566-050-7
ISBN PAPERBACK: 978-1-80566-345-4

## The Puzzle of Existence

Why is the sky so blue today?
And where does my left sock stray?
Is my cat plotting while I nap?
Should I worry or just have a snack?

Questions stack like pancakes high,
Do ducks really swim in the sky?
If I tickle my own feet,
Will the giggles taste like sweet?

## Searching for Shadows

Why do shadows dance at dusk?
Are they sneaky or just a husk?
What's the secret they all know?
Is it to make us laugh or glow?

I chased my shadow down the street,
It ran away, oh what a feat!
Does it have a life of its own?
Or just like me, feels all alone?

## **Timeless Tangles**

Why does time like to twist and twirl?
Is it to make our minds unfurl?
If I could rewind my last mistake,
Would I prefer a big slice of cake?

Days spin round like tops in play,
Do they laugh at what we say?
Could we pause this crazy spree,
And enjoy our tea? Oh, let it be!

## **Labyrinth of Thoughts**

In a maze where thoughts collide,
Do we find truth or just our pride?
With every turn, we question more,
Is the meaning hidden behind the door?

What's the deal with open ends?
Do they lead us to more friends?
In this tangle of curious sights,
Do we find wisdom or just more bites?

## Threads of Life Intertwined

In a great big web of threads,
We trip and fall on borrowed beds.
Questions bounce like balls in play,
Chasing answers that run away.

Why is chocolate sweet yet bitter?
Why do socks always go to glitter?
With laughs, we twist and weave our fate,
In tangled knots, we still create.

## Searching for Stars in the Dark

Under a blanket of night we stare,
Finding stars hidden everywhere.
Is that a wish or just a plane?
Are we all a bit insane?

"Where's the cheese?" one asks aloud,
As if the moon's a creamy crowd.
We giggle at our cosmic plight,
Poking fun at our flawed sight.

## The Looping Carousel of Emotion

Round and round the feelings spin,
Up and down like a quirky grin.
Why is sadness just a phase?
Why do smiles catch us ablaze?

On this ride, we scream and laugh,
Wondering if we should take a bath.
"Life's a circus!" we gleefully claim,
As we juggle joy and a bit of shame.

## **Sifting through Sands of Doubt**

Through grains of doubt, we sift and shake,
Finding treasures, or is that a fake?
Does the sun rise just to tease?
Or is it playing hide and freeze?

As we dig in the sand for clues,
We stumble on some old man's shoes.
In this quest, we laugh and jest,
For life's a puzzle, just like a test.

## Echoes of Eternity

Why do socks disappear, oh dear,
A cosmic game, the missing sphere?
Do aliens wear them in a dance?
Or is it just a laundry chance?

Why do we yawn when everyone's awake?
Is it a signal, or a big mistake?
Like secret codes in silent halls,
Our sleepy calls, oh, how it sprawls!

## **Spirals of Self-Reflection**

Mirror, mirror, who's the fairest?
Is it you or that cactus, hairless?
With every glance, we ponder deep,
Awake or dreaming? Who can keep?

Why do we trip on the very same stair?
Is it fate's joke, or just unfair?
With every stumble, a chuckle's born,
In life's comedy, we're all torn!

## The Dance of Enigmas

What's the secret to joy, I ask?
Is it ice cream or a silly mask?
Is laughter hidden in a cookie,
Or in the shape of a frowning rookie?

Why do we laugh, just to cry?
Is it to see how low we fly?
In every giggle, a riddle swirls,
Life's playful dance, with twirls and whirls!

**Questions Without Borders**

Why do cats knock things off the shelf?
Is it a game, or a cry for help?
With wiggly tails and cosmic might,
They rule the world, both day and night!

What makes our dreams so wild and weird?
Do they come from a place we've feared?
In slumber's realm, we seek and find,
Life's absurd puzzles soothe the mind!

## **Constellations of Doubt and Epiphany**

Stars twinkle, then they fade,
Questions linger, plans are made.
Do socks disappear in space?
Or just vanish without a trace?

Wormholes in the laundry pile,
Time travelers, all in style.
Where's the other half of me?
Oh look, another mystery!

## The Unwritten Story of Eternal Questions

Scribbles on my coffee cup,
Why do we keep filling up?
Pages turning, thoughts collide,
Who wrote this rulebook, and why hide?

Chasing answers like a cat,
Did I leave my keys with that?
Every puzzle piece unmatched,
Life's a riddle, newly hatched!

## A Maze of Thoughts

In the garden of my mind,
Oh, the treasures one can find.
But what to plant, and when to sow?
Wait, is that a weed, or just my woe?

Navigating twists and bends,
Looking for my long-lost friends.
Where's the exit? Oh, there it is!
Just another conundrum, like a quiz!

## Life's Puzzle

Jigsaw pieces, all askew,
Is this sky or ocean blue?
Four corners missing, what a shame,
Where's the fun without the game?

Puzzle piece, forever stray,
Do you know the right ballet?
Twirling clueless on the floor,
Oh wait, there's always room for more!

## Reverberations in the Silence of Query

Echoes bounce in empty halls,
Why does life confuse, enthrall?
Shadows whisper secret tunes,
Of unanswered, floating moons.

In the quiet, thoughts arise,
With a wink and friendly sighs.
Question marks like birds in flight,
Filling up the endless night!

## **Navigating the Abyss**

In a sea of thoughts I float,
Trying to keep my little boat.
Where's the map for all this fuss?
Oh wait, that's just the cat's big bus.

The fish are swimming with a grin,
They know the secrets held within.
I ask them where to cast my line,
They shrug, they just want more sunshine.

## The Quest for Meaning

With a sandwich in my hand, I roam,
Searching for wisdom far from home.
A squirrel yells, 'Ask the tree!'
I nod, but he just wants my brie.

Why do ducks quack, sing, and waddle?
I ponder while I nibble on my model.
A wise old owl blinks, then feigns sleep,
In this game of questions, who's the sheep?

## Tethered to Queries

Tied to questions like a kite,
I soar and swoop, but never quite.
Is there cheese at the end of the maze?
Or just a goat lost in a daze?

I asked a rock, sat down for tea,
It just stared back, 'Look at me!'
So I moved on with my heavy head,
Dreaming of answers that dance instead.

**Unending Fables**

Once a tale began with a jest,
A frog questioned what it means to rest.
He leapt, he croaked, but fell quite flat,
Now he's pondering where his dreams sat.

With toads and tales, we play a game,
Chasing answers without any shame.
I trip over laughter, stumble on fun,
In search of truth, we've barely begun.

## The Riddle of Life Replayed

Why did the chicken stop to think?
Could it be the coffee's too pink?
Round and round, we ask the same
Is this all just a silly game?

Why do socks vanish in the wash?
Perhaps they meet in a secret posh?
Dancing in circles, what a sight,
Oh, life's riddle gives quite a fright!

Do ducks ponder while they quack?
Is there a plan for each raindrop's track?
We'll giggle and grin, the questions fly,
Maybe answers are just a pie in the sky!

Is time a joke played by a clock?
Or just a cat guarding its rock?
Spinning in circles, we laugh and shout,
Life's riddle, oh, what's that all about?

## Repeating Patterns of Existence

Why does toast always land jam-side down?
Could this be fate wearing a frown?
We ponder the crumbs on our plate,
As silly chants make us contemplate.

When does a giraffe check its watch?
Only when lunch is a time to botch!
We spiral through questions big and small,
Like kids on a merry-go-round, we fall.

What if cats secretly rule the night?
While we all dream of endless flight?
Repeating the thoughts that we've tossed,
In patterns of laughter, we count the cost.

Oh, the mysteries of socks and shoes,
Life's silly patterns bring us the blues!
But spirit remains bright and spry,
As we spin and repeat with a wink and a sigh!

## The Echo Chamber of Inquiry

Is pizza a circle or just a pie?
Dough rising high, oh my oh my!
Life echoes laugh out behind closed doors,
As crazy thoughts ring out in roars.

Why do we talk to ourselves in the rain?
Is it the drops or the voice of pain?
Questions bounce back in a playful jest,
As we ponder why we never rest.

Could unicorns be hiding at sea?
Maybe they're sipping sweet herbal tea!
In this chamber, absurdities blend,
With laughter and questions that never end.

Shall we dance with the questions for tea?
Or laugh till we choke at what seems to be?
In every echo, a twist and a turn,
Life's amusing riddles, for those who yearn!

## Unveiling Truths in Circular Pathways

Why does the snail always take its time?
Is it pondering the secrets of rhyme?
In circles it glides, quite slow and sly,
As it wonders why the stars don't fly.

Do fish ever dream of walking on land?
While pondering life with a fin in hand?
In pathways so round, like a loop-de-loop,
We dance through the questions in a silly troupe.

What's the secret behind a dog's bark?
Maybe it's just an amusing lark?
As laughter circles our curious souls,
We unveil the quirks and the comedic roles.

Would a cactus throw a wild party?
Or just poke guests, acting quite hearty?
In circular pathways, we twirl and spin,
Finding truths in laughter, where we begin!

# Reflections in the Waters of Time

In a pond, my face does float,
Is that a fish, or just a goat?
I squint and stare, what do I see?
Just ripples laughing back at me.

The frog croaks out a wise old thing,
"Why chase the future?" he does sing.
"Look at the bugs who hop and fly,
They ponder little, and then just try!"

The sun peeks down, with rays so bright,
It asks me if I've brushed my bite.
I scratch my head, and then I say,
"Maybe tomorrow, I'll start today."

"Oh time, oh time, why were you late?
You can't blame me for the small plate.
I'm going in circles, can't you see?
Even the clock laughs right at me."

# The Spiral of Perception and Understanding

Around and around, I spin my dreams,
In circles tight, or so it seems.
Questions whirl like leaves in fall,
Do they mean something? Not at all.

Socks without pairs, oh where do they go?
Into the void, or just for show?
My mind's a maze of mismatched thoughts,
Like trying to count a hundred dots.

"Wisdom comes through trial," they said,
As I tripped on my laces and fell on my head.
But who was wise, and who was fool?
Maybe I'm both; now that's the rule!

Eyes wide open, I grab a chair,
And ponder why I can't find hair.
In this spiral of questions galore,
I land on answers—then ask for more!

## Whispers in the Hall of Mirrors

In a hall where echoes play,
Reflections giggle, dance, and sway.
I wave to me and laugh aloud,
Only to greet the silliest crowd.

"Who's the fairest?" one mirror said,
But its frame seemed to shake its head.
With all this banter, the ghosts might swoon,
Whispering secrets that make no tune.

As I stumble through my own bright face,
Does the world even know its place?
In every twist, confusion reigns,
Though I'm certain I just found my gains!

So here's to questions in every glance,
With each new line, there's room to dance.
In a hall of mirrors, let's lose track,
And ask those questions—who needs a map?

## Questions: The Seeds of Contemplation

In a garden of thoughts where ideas bloom,
Each seed asks loudly, "What's my room?"
Water me, sunshine, and maybe fate,
Let's sprout some queries, it'll be great!

Is a cat a fish, or a rat in disguise?
The plants just giggle at my surprise.
Do veggies argue, or is it a myth?
In this plot, let's dig deep, I'll find out the truth!

"Who's the boss of the busy bee?"
The blooms all smile, and chorus with glee.
For in this patch of pondering green,
Life's just a riddle wrapped in a bean.

So plant your questions, watch them grow,
In this wild garden, we'll steal the show.
For every query that springs from dread,
Could be the magic that takes us ahead!

## Tides of Inquiry

Why do socks go missing in the wash?
Are they off to start a party? Oh my gosh!
Do they dance with dust bunnies in a spree?
Or just plot revenge on you and me?

Why do lighters always play hide and seek?
Do they think being lost makes them unique?
Or is it just a game of cosmic fun?
As we search for them, the chase has begun.

Is cereal soup, if you add some milk?
Or just breakfast's version, smooth as silk?
If a tree falls, does it truly make sound?
Or just echo away, lost and unbound?

What's the purpose of a rubber band?
Is it there to hold dreams or to be bland?
Life's questions roll in waves with a sigh,
In this comical quest, we all just fly!

## **Boundless Waves of Thought**

Why do we think about what's for dinner?
When yesterday's leftovers, they seem a winner?
Do forks hold secrets that spoons cannot share?
In kitchens of chaos, do they form a square?

Why does the cake always taste so divine?
Even a slice makes the sun seem to shine?
Is it magic or just sugar in play?
Or does it speak truths that life can't relay?

If cats really ruled, what laws would they make?
No doggy doors opened, just naps and some cake?
Would they demand tuna and soft comfy beds?
While humans serve snacks by their furry heads?

Why do we ponder the mysteries of fate?
Does it come on a plate, or do we just wait?
In this sea of thoughts, we endlessly drift,
With laughter as sails, we embrace every lift!

## Kaleidoscope of Queries

Why do we ask why, in circles we go?
Questions like confetti, they flutter and flow,
Is the universe laughing at our endless plight?
Or is it just bored under the stars at night?

Why do umbrellas invert in the rain?
Do they think it's a game, a dance of disdain?
Is weather just nature's way to play tricks?
While we dash like madmen, dodging the kicks?

Do we truly understand what a meme does mean?
Or is it just laughter displayed on a screen?
If a cat plays piano, is he signing a deal?
In the whims of this world, it's a surreal reel!

With each twist and turn, our thoughts intertwine,
A colorful puzzle, both silly and fine,
Life asks us questions we ponder and fling,
In this hilarious dance, oh, let's laugh and sing!

## Reflections in a Still Pool

Why do we stare at our own reflection?
Searching for answers in every direction?
Is the person we see really quite true?
Or just a fun house mirror with a view?

If time could talk, what tales would it share?
Would it gossip about people, feathers, and hair?
Or tell us the secrets of moments we've bled,
As it tick-tocks away, weaving jokes in our head?

Why do we chase after dreams that are fleeting?
Is it the thrill of the chase that keeps us beating?
Do stars hide in our hearts, waiting to shine?
In this hilarious pursuit, we're all intertwined!

Questions like bubbles float up to the sky,
Popping with laughter as they flutter by,
With joy in our hearts, let's dance through the night,
In this playful abyss, oh, what a delight!

## **Ever-Looping Quest of the Mind**

Why do socks always go astray?
They vanish like dreams at break of day.
Mind twists and turns, oh what a sight,
Chasing thoughts that dance in the light.

Why does ice cream melt in the sun?
Like life's big questions, never done.
Taste buds argue, sweet battles rage,
While I scribble notes on an old page.

Why do we step on each other's toes?
In this jumbled dance, who really knows?
Twists and turns, a merry-go-round,
Falling and laughing, it's joy we've found.

Why do we ponder through day and night?
With each question leads to new insight.
In the circus of thoughts, we're all a part,
Struggling for answers but laughing from the heart.

## Unraveling the Mystery of Existence

What came first, the chicken or the egg?
Philosophers ponder and writers beg.
While the rooster crows, we scratch our heads,
Creating odd theories and silly threads.

Is it true that cats see ghosts at play?
Or is it all just a feline cliché?
With their twitching tails and haunted stares,
I'm left to wonder while pulling my hair.

If we talk to plants, do they understand?
Do daisies listen as we make demands?
In whispers of leaves, a chuckle is heard,
As we converse softly with every word.

Why do we ask, yet rarely decide?
In this quest for truth, we laugh and hide.
With each puzzling riddle that comes into view,
Life's a grand joke, we're the punchline too.

## Reflections in a Timeless Pool

When gazing deep into a still pond,
Do fish ponder dreams or just respond?
Are they planning escapes or just having fun?
Perhaps they're plotting under the sun.

Mirrors of water, what do they see?
Reflections of life's absurdity.
The frogs croak wisdom in goofy tongues,
While the dragonflies dance like tiny bungs.

Why do we seek what's perfectly true?
When reality often feels askew.
With laughter and quirks, we navigate fate,
Finding joy in the chaos, never too late.

With every ripple, another thought bubbles,
Each splash brings laughter amidst life's troubles.
As we gaze at our questions in each wave's curl,
We can't help but laugh at this topsy world.

## Cycles of Wonder

Why do we chase down every clue?
In circles we run, look, there's déjà vu!
The hamster wheel of thoughts spins around,
While we giggle in madness, we're never profound.

If life's a roller coaster, where's the thrill?
Why do we scream when we're on the hill?
With every twist, we grasp for the sky,
Yet losing our minds, we just laugh and cry.

Why does the clock always seem to laugh?
Tick-tock, it teases our humble path.
In the party of time where giggles reside,
We dance between seasons, hearts open wide.

With wonders in cycles, what's the grand task?
To laugh at the questions, and happily bask.
For in life's funny dance, we find our way,
Through cycles of wonder, we play every day.

## **Cycles of Search**

What's hiding behind that closet door?
Old clothes and shoes, maybe something more?
As I search for meaning, I trip on a shoe,
Life's messiness shows through, it's true!

Is happiness found in a perfectly neat space?
Or in socks with holes, in the warm embrace?
As I dig through the clutter, I giggle and shout,
For life is a riddle, and that's what it's about.

Why do we ponder when we should just eat?
A slice of good cake can't be beat!
In the cycle of search for what brings us cheer,
Chocolate and laughter are always near.

With questions aplenty and answers so few,
In cycles of search, the absurd shines through.
As we dodge the serious, we kick off our shoes,
In the dance of existence, it's fun that we choose.

## Chasing Fleeting Answers

Why is the sky so blue today?
A parrot said, 'Go ask the sun!'
But wait, I forgot what I would say—
The clues just seem to weigh a ton.

I searched the fridge for wisdom here,
Found only leftovers, cold and stale.
The milk told me to switch to beer,
But I don't think that's a holy grail!

Strolling through the park, I muse,
A squirrel laughs, 'What's wrong with you?'
I toss a nut, the answer blues,
Yet more questions come into view!

So here I sit, a puzzled chap,
The ducks just quack and waddle past,
They know the secret to this trap,
But I'm too busy to ask fast.

## **Infinity's Riddle**

In a world where socks disappear,
Mysteries wrapped in laundry lore,
I ponder why they cause such fear,
And giggle at what came before.

Is cheese more wise than ancient sage?
A mouse would claim it holds the key,
But I'm stuck here at this stage,
Debating snacks with brie and camembert tea!

The cat just yawns, 'You're wasting time,'
'Just chase a ball and join the fun!'
Yet here I am, lost in this rhyme,
Searching for answers 'til I'm done.

So round and round, I twist and spin,
Chasing riddles like a fool,
But the joy is where I begin,
In this playground of bizarre rule.

## Resonance of the Unasked

What happens when toast hits the floor?
Do the fairies laugh or simply sigh?
Today I ponder, wanting more,
While the dog just cocks his eye.

If grass had feelings, what would it say?
'Cut me, don't cut me, oh dear friend!'
But I just munch, because it's hay,
And in this chaos, giggles blend!

The mirror winks with secrets bold,
'Have you asked why you wear that hat?'
I realize now, I'm just the mold,
In this fashion of questioning spat!

But in this maze of silly thought,
I find a rhythm, a funky beat,
Laughter blooms from answers sought,
In this dance of joy, I'm complete!

## The Cycle of Wonder

Why do my shoes always feel tight?
Are my feet growing, or is it me?
I question life late at night,
While snoring cats laugh silently.

Where do the missing keys go hide?
Perhaps they live in Narnia's maze?
A cookie jar might be their guide,
In dreams they dance in sugary haze!

Time travels by on a floppy disk,
'Take a selfie,' my phone just chirps.
In this moment, it's quite the risk,
Yet here I stand, among the burps!

So round I go, with thoughts anew,
Finding joy in playful digs,
For in this circus, it's all true,
Life's a laugh, just watch the gigs!

## **Reflections in a Broken Mirror**

In a mirror cracked, I see my face,
A puzzling smile, a strange embrace.
Questions dance like ants on a hill,
Why is time so odd, and yet so still?

I ask my socks, where do you flee?
One ends up lost, two is a spree.
The cat just yawns, no answers in sight,
Should I take a nap or stay up all night?

Eyes wide open, I wonder and blink,
Is pizza a snack, or do we overthink?
Life's little quirks keep me on my toes,
Why do we laugh? Only the mirror knows.

A broken glass, yet it's all so clear,
Questions abound, but I'll drink my beer.
With laughter and joy, I wade through the mess,
Are we all just jesters, more or less?

## Echoes of Unanswered Puzzles

In a room full of echoes, the walls start to hum,
Seeking the answer, I just feel so dumb.
Where do lost socks go? What's hiding in there?
My brain's a jungle, filled with wild hair.

Why do I trip on things that aren't there?
Questions abound, but who really cares?
An ice cream cone melts, is it sad or not?
Maybe it's thinking of all it forgot.

A chicken inquires, "Why cross the road?"
To get to the punchline, or lighten the load?
The rabbit just chuckles, still late to the show,
In this grand game of life, what's left to know?

With laughter like confetti, we float through the air,
Puzzles keep coming, but we're all unaware.
In a world of giggles, we twirl and we spin,
The quest for the answers is where we begin.

## Spiraling Through the Mind's Maze

In a maze of thoughts, I turn left and right,
Searching for answers that hide out of sight.
Where's my other shoe? I just had it before,
Is there a sock thief that I should ignore?

Whispers of wisdom float by like a breeze,
Why do I laugh when I trip on my knees?
The plants in the corner lean in for a peek,
Do they have secrets or just love to squeak?

Round and round, like a merry-go-round,
Questions tickle my brain, but what have I found?
A hamster's wheel spins as I sip my tea,
Is it me, or the tea that's just too fancy?

With each twist and turn, I may lose my mind,
But running in circles can be quite the find.
So here's to the riddles that make us feel spry,
In this whimsical maze, we laugh as we fly.

# An Eternal Search for Meaning

With a magnifying glass, I peer at the ants,
What's their great mission? Do they throw dance plans?
Do they ponder the stars while gathering crumbs?
Or are they just experts at dodging my thumbs?

Why do we giggle when we spill our drinks?
Is it the thrill, or the way that it stinks?
A cosmic question just waiting to sprout,
Do fish ever wish for a night out in clouds?

While standing in line for some pancakes and jam,
I ponder my existence, perhaps with a lamb.
Is meaning a pancake, flat, round, and sweet?
Or is it the topping that makes life complete?

So here we are, in this carnival ride,
Questions like popcorn, no need to hide.
In laughter and joy, we find what's not seen,
In this playful world, we stay evergreen.

## A Tapestry of Unsolved Mysteries

In a world where socks go missing,
Lost beneath the sofa's grace,
We ponder fate and fate's dismissing,
Where's my other sock? Not a trace!

Questions float like balloons in air,
Why do toasters always burn,
As we scratch our heads in despair,
A lesson here—shall we not learn?

Why is cereal treated with glee,
Only to drown in a milky sea?
Who knew breakfast brought such a spree,
So much joy, yet so much mystery!

In every giggle, laughter's sway,
Life asks odd things on a whim,
We laugh, we cry, we play all day,
And still, the answers stay quite dim!

**The Cycle of Seeking and Finding**

Why's the cat the king of the house?
Strutting 'round like a noble bird,
With dignity—like a quiet mouse,
    All absent of a single word.

Why's the fridge a midnight lure,
Holding secrets no one should know?
With cold pizza, it feels so pure,
In the dark where dreams do flow.

In the quest for snacks, oh what a fight,
    Why do chips always vanish fast?
    Chasing crumbs, we feel delight,
    Life's little puzzles, unsurpassed!

Yet amidst the giggles and the frowns,
We chase the truth with playful glee,
Always spinning round like clowns,
    And finding joy in the mystery!

## Labyrinth of Thoughts Unwinding

In a maze of thoughts, oh so grand,
Where did I put my favorite book?
I search with care and feel quite banned,
From logic's grip—what a strange hook!

Why do we ask the same old things,
As if answers grow on trees?
Why not simply sprout some wings,
And sail through life on a playful breeze?

Every riddle's just a roundabout,
Why did I walk into that room?
With a smile, I laugh and shout,
I've forgotten—oh, well, I'll zoom!

In the twisting paths of thought's delight,
We laugh at questions blurring sight,
Chasing shadows 'til we find the light,
Life's a puzzle, a glorious sight!

## The Quest for Answers Never Ceasing

What's the deal with socks and shoes?
Their mates are lost in wardrobe land,
We search for pairs and often lose,
While mismatched styles are just so grand!

Why does coffee spill at dawn?
As sleepy heads begin to brew,
Is it a prank or fate withdrawn?
A miracle or just bad luck too?

Why do we wander in our dreams,
Pondering thoughts like treasure maps?
With coffee cups, we chase moonbeams,
And answerless thoughts lead to mishaps!

Yet in the chaos, laughter thrives,
As questions dance on every page,
In this wild mix of silly lives,
We find our joy—pure, strong, and sage!

## Paradoxes in Perpetual Motion

Why do we park in driveways, oh so wide?
Yet we drive on parkways, it's a crazy ride!
Should I eat the leftover cake in delight?
Or save it for later, out of sheer fright?

In a world full of riddles, questions abound,
Why do lost socks never seem to be found?
Is a round pizza served in a square box?
And why don't we question all the talking clocks?

Do fish get thirsty? A thought that's absurd!
And if space is empty, why isn't it heard?
Must we always repeat what we say to the cat?
Or can we just let them figure out where we're at?

Why is it we call it rush hour, you see?
When no one is rushing, just sipping their tea?
And when do we stop this amusing charade?
Perhaps, my dear friend, when we learn to upgrade!

## Constellations of Unanswered Queries

Why do we press harder on the remote at night?
When the battery's dead, nothing can take flight?
How do we find our keys, always misplaced?
Yet we look for lost thoughts, with sublime grace?

If a turtle loses its shell, is it naked or not?
When does a joke become funny or forgot?
Why do we drive with our hands on the wheel?
When steering with thoughts seems a better deal?

Why are there so many dishes to wash, I fear?
But we make the same mess with each holiday cheer?
Do we really need all these channels in sight?
When all we want is to binge-watch till light?

What if the moon was just cheese, oh what glee!
Imagine the parties, the cosmic jubilee!
Why not just dance under starlit affection?
Let's take a spin in this whimsical direction!

## A Melody of Endless Questions

Why is it called a building when it's already built?
And what's with those moments that make us feel guilt?
Do vegetables play hide and seek in the fridge?
While dreaming of freedom, maybe a bridge?

In a world so vast, does time really exist?
Or is it just a plot twist we've all missed?
Why do store doors say push or pull?
When all we really want is ice cream, oh so cool?

Are we more awake when we yield to the dream?
Or less aware when making life's scheme?
Does coffee really wake us, or is it just fate?
That stirs us to ponder, and sometimes just wait?

Why do we laugh, but then question the rhyme?
In these zany musings, we dance with our time!
Shall we hum the tune of the wacky and bright?
For here in our questions, the world feels just right!

## Fragments of Thought in Constant Flux

Why do we call it a rush if we're nearly late?
And how come the snacks disappear off my plate?
Do shadows have secrets that only we miss?
Or do whispers of wonder, blend in with bliss?

Is it odd that we toast to what's yet to arrive?
While dreaming of futures that barely survive?
If we trip on the sidewalk, is it part of a joke?
Or are our feet laughing, just setting the yoke?

Why do we chase what we cannot quite see?
When the answers are hidden inside you and me?
Is a pencil broken when it can't leave a mark?
Or does it just choose to go out with a spark?

In a whirl of ideas, let's play with the art!
Of weaving our thoughts into laughter and heart!
For within these odd queries, we find some delight,
In the strands of this life, ever wiggly and bright!

## Threads of Curiosity Weaving Complexity

In the cupboard of dreams, what's hiding?
Is it socks with a fate undeciding?
Jelly beans solve problems, or so they claim,
But who's the genius to decide their name?

Do fish wear glasses when they swim?
Is that why the ocean seems so dim?
Questions dangle like lights on a tree,
Twinkling wildly, asking, 'What's next for me?'

Are clouds but cotton candy in disguise?
While squirrels plot world domination, oh my!
I ponder as I sip on my tea,
What do they whisper in the next grand spree?

With each thread tangled, we weave anew,
Making patterns we barely construe.
In this fabric of strange, let's take a spin,
Laughing at how wild curiosity's been!

## Chasing Shadows of Knowledge

Why does my shadow dance in delight?
It's probably plotting my next snack bite.
Does it dream of pizza or maybe cake?
Perhaps it's just bored; oh, for goodness' sake!

Each time I seek answers, they scatter like flies,
Chasing them feels like a circus surprise.
The more that I ponder, the clearer it gets,
My thoughts are like kittens with no etiquette.

What if cats ruled the world and we just cook?
Would they write an epic or read a good book?
With tails held high, they'd slap down the rules,
Declaring their reign from the sky, as the fools!

So grab your magnifying glass, let's explore,
This silly chase opens every door.
With shadows leading the way on this quest,
We'll find that the search is what we love best!

## The Perpetual Dance of Wonder

Why do we step on cracks in the street?
Are we tiptoeing through whimsical heat?
The rhythm of life plays a jaunty tune,
With questions that bounce like a bright-bright moon.

When socks go missing, what's their fate?
Do they party with spoons on a dinner plate?
The dance of the silly, the waltz of the vague,
Inquiring minds jump on this footloose stage.

If ducks wore bow ties, would they quack with style?
Or would they still waddle and just beguile?
Each question waltzes on a loop so grand,
Tickling our senses; we hardly can stand.

So pull on your shoes, let's cut the rug,
Laughing through life like a playful bug.
In the dance of it all, we spin and sway,
Finding joy in inquiry, come what may!

## Questions That Loop Like a River

Why does my dog bark at the moonlit glow?
As if it's the best joke he'll ever know.
Each woof is a question without any clue,
While I ponder on why I missed my shoe!

When do the starlings decide to unite?
Is there a meeting every Thursday night?
They gossip and tweet, oh what a wild scene,
Plotting their flight paths to spots unseen.

If spaghetti could talk, what tales would it share?
Would it spill secrets like confetti in air?
Noodles twist stories of triumph and woe,
But perhaps that's a thought we should let go.

So here we are, on a riverside stroll,
Frolicking questions, they capture our soul.
In the loop of our thoughts, laughter flows free,
Dancing with questions, just you and me!

## Moments Captured in a Glass Sphere

A thought just popped, like bubble gum,
It bursts with joy, then leaves me numb.
I ponder deep, then I forget,
What was that question? I'm not sure yet!

A squirrel danced by, with nuts in tow,
Completing a riddle I didn't know.
I ask him why he's in such a rush,
He twitches his tail, in a playful hush.

A cat nearby, with a smug little grin,
Looks at my plight, as if to win.
"If you find the answer, do share the taste!"
I laugh and cry, life's a funny haste!

So here I sip from this glassy sphere,
Chasing questions, but hold them dear.
Each little moment, a chance to spin,
What's life without laughter in this din?

## The Quest for Clarity Amidst Chaos

I sought for wisdom in the fridge,
Found a leftover cake, well, check the ridge!
Is frosting a question? A universal one?
I swear that slice of pie just did run!

The dog barks loud, as if to say,
"Hey, buddy, life's just a game we play!"
I scratch my head, is he right or wrong?
With barks and bites, the quest goes long.

A sock went missing, was it ever there?
Maybe it hid, to avoid despair?
Am I asking too much from laundry's spin?
Life's tales unfold with a cheeky grin.

Amidst this chaos, thoughts swirl around,
Each question, a giggle, a truth that's bound.
In the messy kitchen, I find delight,
Clarity hides where the dust takes flight!

## Conundrums Paint the Canvas of Life

A painter stands with color so bright,
Wondering why blue feels just right.
With each brush stroke, questions ignite,
Is that the moon, or just me at night?

The canvas laughs, it tells no lies,
"Your doubts are simply echoes of sighs."
A dog in the corner seems to agree,
Nibbling at nothing, full of glee.

My pencil snapped, oh what a mess!
Can broken things bring happiness?
With every fracture, a new design,
Is chaos just art in another line?

As colors mix and fade away,
The paradox dances, come what may.
In conundrums painted, life's truths unfurl,
In laughter, we twirl, in this funny whirl!

## Whirls of Thought Entangled in Context

In circles I run, thoughts cross and twine,
Like spaghetti noodles on a kitchen line.
"Why are we here?" a goat once bleated,
While I just sat, and my tea retreated.

The clock ticks louder, each tick a tease,
"Was that a question?" Oh, if you please!
But dogs bark louder, as if they know,
In whirls of thought, we dance and flow.

I ponder deep while juggling socks,
Can puzzles give answers? Or just paradox?
Each twist and turn, a giggly leap,
In tangled thoughts, the answers creep.

So swirling I go, in my cozy chair,
Baffled by questions that float in the air.
Entangled in context, life's grand ballet,
We find life's meaning, in a humorous play!

## Questions Blossoming in the Garden of the Mind

Why does a donut look like the sun?
Is that why we eat them, just for fun?
Are flowers talking in colors so bright?
Or are they whispering secrets at night?

Do bees take a break, or do they just hum?
What if their buzz is their way to succumb?
Can grass feel the tickle when we walk through?
Or does it just laugh, thinking 'Achoo'?

Is laughter a plant that grows in the air?
How does it spread? Is it really quite rare?
If wisdom is gold, then where's the machine?
To churn out the nuggets we're yet to glean?

Can clouds play hopscotch, or do they just float?
Does the moon need a boat, or can it just gloat?
With nature in question, all tangled and fun,
Let's ask funny things, till the day is done!

## Circular Roads of Philosophy Untraveled

If we're lost in thought, who has the map?
Or is it in circles that we're prone to nap?
Does wisdom come cheap, or is it a sale?
With every decision, do we just derail?

Is time a buffet where seconds all serve?
Do moments dance awkwardly, lacking reserve?
And when do you know if you've found the truth?
When it starts wearing socks with holes since youth?

Is the meaning of life just a roundabout?
Where all roads diverge, filled with laughter and doubt?
Or do philosophers trip on their own shoe?
Chasing conclusions that lead them askew?

Can pondering donuts lead to the pie?
Or will we just end up with sprinkles to try?
In this wacky parade of thoughts on a whim,
Let's giggle and ponder, on the edge—let's swim!

## The Puzzle of Being and Becoming

Does being a toaster give it a sense?
Is its job just to warm, or is that too dense?
What if a chair could write its own book?
Would it talk about cushions and how they look?

As people transform, is change a charade?
Are we just actors on time's silly stage?
If life's a great puzzle, where's the missing piece?
Could it be the socks that we lost in the fleece?

Are jellybeans aware of their sweet little fate?
Are they nervous, or do they sit back and wait?
When we peel back the layers of who we are,
Do we find a mystery, or just a candy bar?

With questions like bubbles, just floating around,
Let's pop them with laughter, see where we're bound.
In this quirky dance of becoming and be,
Every inquiry tickles, and so let's just see!

## Echoes of Tomorrow in Today's Questions

If tomorrow's a party, where is the invite?
Are balloons built from wishes that take flight?
Do stars need a nap when the sun sets low?
Or do they just play hide and seek with the glow?

Is yesterday's laughter a sound that can grow?
Or do we just keep it on old vinyl records that slow?
Can wishes from dreams become actual things?
Or are they just whispers that the night brings?

What if our shadows are people we know?
Or maybe they're just friends in a light show?
If today is a sandwich, do we bite with glee?
If we add extra questions, how tasty will be?

As echoes of joy bounce from future to now,
Let's munch on the questions and ponder the how.
With giggles and grins, let the queries unfold,
For in every inquiry, a new story told!

## **Parables in a Spiral Dance**

Round and round the questions spin,
In circles like a dizzy grin.
Why is the chicken crossing roads?
For giggles, laughs, and all that codes!

Turtles wear their homes so proud,
While rabbits hop, a bouncing crowd.
Do fish ever get the urge to fly?
Just for fun, they'll surely try!

When planets dance, do they ask why?
For cosmic laughs, they twirl and sigh.
Is time a line, or a drippy mess?
Pour it in a cup, I guess!

So twirl and whirl, let questions play,
In this wild game, we laugh away.
For every answer, a quirky twist,
In this spiral dance, how can we resist?

## **Pages of a Never-Ending Story**

Flip a page, then turn it back,
What's the point? I seem to lack!
Did the cat really wear those boots?
Or are they just dressing for the loot?

Once upon a time, it seems,
The toaster had delicious dreams.
Can a sock find its sole mate?
Or do they just procrastinate?

Heroes trip on their own capes,
As villains hide behind the drapes.
What's the plot twist we all crave?
Maybe it's a dance, so brave!

So laugh with me through every line,
In this story, all's divine.
For every ending seeks a start,
In the book of life, we play our part.

**Visions Flitting Like Butterflies**

Butterflies ask where the blooms go,
As they flutter to and fro.
Do clouds ever ponder their fluff?
Or just float around, never tough?

Worms make tunnels; do they complain?
"Hey, I'm bored! Can we change terrain?"
The sun giggles, "I'm on my way,
To light up your dark, don't you sway!"

Squirrels debate on the best nut,
While pigeons coo, "We're in a rut!"
What makes a rainbow bend and sway?
Perhaps it just wants to play!

Life's a dance with questions bright,
Flitting by like wings in flight.
Let's chase them down until we tire,
And laugh at questions we all desire!

## The Fabric of Questions Woven Tight

Threads of wonder, woven neat,
In a fabric of thoughts, oh so sweet.
Why do socks always lose their pairs?
Must they wander off to secret lairs?

A tapestry filled with color bold,
Each stitch a story waiting to unfold.
Do snakes question their slippery fate?
Or just slide by, feeling great?

The sun's a painter, drops of gold,
On a canvas, vivid and uncontrolled.
Can shadows giggle in the night?
Or do they flee from morning light?

So wear this quilt of queries bright,
Embrace the strange, the weird delight.
In every question, a tale resides,
In the fabric of life, fun collides!

# Answers Lost in the Tides of Time

Waves crash while thoughts drift away,
Wondering where those lost dreams stay.
Questions like fish, swim to and fro,
There's a net somewhere, but where? Who knows!

Clock hands twirl like dancers in jest,
Each tick a query, a curious quest.
We ask, we laugh, forget what was said,
Then trip on the answers we never could thread.

Sandcastles crumble, the tides are cruel,
But building them keeps us feeling a fool.
The seashells whisper secrets so sweet,
Yet they vanish too fast, get swept off their feet.

Maybe we just need a wide-open smile,
To swim through the questions, oh, what a trial!
The tide's on our side, let's go for a ride,
Laughing at answers that slip like the tide.

## The Kaleidoscope of Yearning

Colors spin in a laughter's spree,
Each turn reveals what we wish to see.
Frustrated dreams in the light start to twirl,
Can't catch a glimpse of that platinum pearl!

Hearts like rainbows, racing to blend,
Each hue a question, does it ever end?
Oh what a circus, this life that we chase,
Hoping for answers, yet finding a face.

With every shift in this dazzling view,
We ponder and wonder, both me and you.
Are our questions just shadows that play?
Bouncing in circles, hip hip hooray!

Laughter erupts, as we ponder in glee,
What colors await for you and me.
In the kaleidoscope twist, we roll with the fun,
In this merry go round, we've only begun!

## The Enigma of Existence

What's the meaning of life in a cookie's crunch?
Is it hiding in crumbs when we munch?
Mysteries flutter like moths in the night,
But surely, they giggle at our baffled fright.

We ask the stars, they just blink with a grin,
Maybe the answers are tucked in within.
Like socks missing partners, we search and we seek,
For a wink from the cosmos or maybe a freak!

Questions parade in a comical march,
"Why do we trip on a tree root? March!"
Existence may jest, like a jester so sly,
Yet we chase after answers, aiming high.

So here's to life's mysteries, wrapped up in cheer,
Maybe we'll find the truth, or just a cold beer.
Let's laugh at the puzzles that tickle our minds,
For in the grand scheme, laughter forever binds!

## Cerulean Skies of Wondering Souls

Above our heads, the cerulean vast,
Clouds float like dreams, fading too fast.
We gaze at the heavens, searching for clues,
Is there a map we have all yet to lose?

With every puff of cotton candy air,
We ponder our place, our fortunes, and dare.
The birds chirp questions that flit on the breeze,
Do they know the secrets hidden in trees?

As sunshine dances on whimsical trails,
We scribble our doubts in fanciful tales.
What if the answers were just a few laughs?
Or waiting in fields, in whimsical drafts?

So let's leap through the clouds, arms wide in delight,
Embracing the wonders that burst into sight.
In cerulean skies where our hopes intertwine,
We'll find joy in questions, like the finest wine!

## The Dance of Curiosity and Doubt

In a room full of chairs, I found a sock,
It stared at me silently, just like a clock.
Questions spun round in a dizzying trance,
Why do we wear shoes when we can't even dance?

A cat on the roof, what is he thinking?
Maybe of fish or his neighbor's blinking.
I toss him a question, he flicks his tail,
Does he ponder the future or a catfood sale?

A pickle jar sits, sealed tight with a grin,
What secrets it holds? Let the tasting begin!
Is it sour or sweet? Oh, what a debate,
I dive in with courage to challenge my fate.

When will we learn, the answers are fun?
Like socks with no matches, they disappear one by one.
Life's a funny puzzle, bits scattered about,
Let's dance with the queries, giggle, and shout!

## Whirligigs of the Heart and Mind

A thought like a whirlwind, it spins and it swirls,
Like a girl in a dress, with a dance and twirl.
I asked my reflection, who are you today?
It winked back in jest, then turned to ballet!

A cloud on a whim, it rumbled and tossed,
Where do you go when your fluffiness is lost?
To rain on the world or simply to float,
I followed it home, in a tiny boat!

Thoughts come like popcorn, popping with glee,
What flavor is wisdom? Is it sweet or free?
A kernel of doubt sits by the popcorn pot,
But each burst's a giggle, a joy we forgot!

With hearts made of jelly, we bounce and we rhyme,
In this circus of life, there's no need for time.
So let's juggle our worries beneath the big top,
Laughing and spinning until we all drop!

# Beyond the Horizon of Certainties

A chicken crossed over, oh what a bold quest,
To reach the other side or just take a rest?
It pondered the risks, should I hop or would flinch?
For every bold answer, there comes a tight clinch!

In dreams of big whales and tiny old ants,
I sought out the reason, and they all did dance.
An elephant trumpets, in colorful style,
What's better than coffee? It pondered a while!

Invisible doubts dance around in the night,
Like fireflies laughing, oh what a sight!
They twirled through my thoughts, a confusing parade,
As I chased them with questions, unafraid, unfrayed.

Through mirages of wisdom, we navigate air,
On waves of absurdity, there's laughter to spare.
So let's sail to tomorrow on questions and hearts,
For every great answer is where the fun starts!

## Waves of Thought in Continuous Motion

A fish in a pond thinks it's swimming in space,
What if that splash is just a ticklish embrace?
It flips and it flops, with a wink in its fin,
Am I the fish, or is the pond thick with kin?

Clouds race above on a bright sunny day,
Are they chasing the wind or just learning to play?
With each little puff comes a giggle or two,
Oh look, I just caught a whimsy, it's you!

Thoughts rumble like thunder, but rain never drops,
Should I dance in the puddles or hop on the hops?
With laughter like bubbles, I float through the air,
Confetti of musings in moments so rare.

So here's to the twirls of our minds on a ride,
Let's splash in the questions, let joy be our guide.
Each wave flows with fun, in a sea full of cheer,
With every mad venture, we hold life quite dear!

## Shadows Danced by Flickering Flames

Shadows waltz under the moon's bright gaze,
Their silly jig brings laughter and craze.
They spin and twirl with a comical flair,
While marvelling at secrets floating in air.

A cat takes a bow, then pursues a chase,
While echoes of questions dive into space.
Is it the flame or the shadows that yawn?
Who knows where the dawn will be leading us on?

With each flicker, a thought takes its flight,
Why is it darkness that hovers at night?
Who needs the answers when jokes make us grin?
Let's tickle the fates and embrace the spin!

So let's dance with the doubts, sway with the light,
For shadows are funny when fears are in sight.
In the flickering glow, laughter will reign,
As we prance through the questions, a merry refrain.

## Questions that Bloom and Wither

In the garden of whims, questions take root,
Some bloom like bright flowers, others, a hoot.
Why do we giggle when tripping on air?
Is laughter a flower or just a wild scare?

With petals unfurling, their colors so bold,
Inquiries sprout, both timid and old.
Can daisies answer the meaning of bliss?
Or will their confessions be lost in the mist?

But there stands a wise old bee, buzzing near,
Claiming to know the answers we fear.
"Why not just pollinate thoughts in your mind?
When questions come blooming, just unwind, unwind!"

So we'll party with blooms, let our laughter take flight,
As the sun dips below, turning day into night.
With questions keep rising, let's dance with the breeze,
In this garden of nonsense, let's do as we please!

## The Veil of Uncertainty Lifts and Falls

A veil flutters gently, teasing the wise,
Hiding the answers, full of surprise.
Why are socks missing? Where do they go?
What secrets do mirrors hide just below?

With each lift and drop, the questions collide,
Like ducks in a row, they stumble, they slide.
Will we find the answers, or just a lost sock?
Oh, the gossip they share when we're out for a walk!

Amidst chuckles and giggles, the veil swings wide,
Taunting us gently, like waves on a tide.
If knowledge is power, why does it flee?
Perhaps it's the puzzle that sets us all free!

So let's dance with the veil, let our minds have their say,
For without all the questions, who'd want it that way?
In this humorous mess, our laughter will crawl,
Through every layer, we'll giggle and sprawl!

## Inquiries in the Garden of Existence

In a garden of whims, the questions sprout,
With tiny umbrellas, they wiggle about.
Can a cucumber ponder its place in the stew?
Or will broccoli muse on the riddle of blue?

A sunflower whispers, "I'm tall for a reason,
To gaze at the skies through each joyful season!"
But what of the weeds, so tangled and spry?
Are they crafty philosophers just passing by?

As clouds drift above, we ponder in jest,
Do plants ever dream? Do they know they're the best?
What's life without laughter, a garden so bare?
With giggles and questions, we'll color the air!

So join in the fun, let's waltz with the green,
For existence, my friend, is a whimsical scene.
In the garden of jest, let inquiries sway,
And we'll laugh our way through each curious day!

## Endless Reflections

I asked a mirror what it saw,
It laughed and said, 'Just flaws!'
I wondered why it made me frown,
Then it cracked up and fell down.

Why does the sun rise every day?
Is it just to make me sway?
I scratched my head in bright sunlight,
Then tripped and fell, oh what a sight!

I pondered why clouds float so high,
Are they shy or just too fly?
They winked at me, then rained instead,
So I chased them off and went to bed.

In circles I twirl, round and round,
Chasing answers that can't be found.
But laughter echoes, my heart's delight,
In this silly game of day and night.

## Circles of Curiosity

Why do cats sit in a box?
Do they think it's a paradox?
I asked the dog, he just sighed,
As he lay down and slowly dried.

What if trees could actually talk?
Would they gossip or just squawk?
I chased a squirrel, it flicked its tail,
Laughing hard, I forgot my trail.

Is grass jealous of the sky?
Does it wish to give clouds a try?
I kicked a stone and watched it bounce,
While ants danced in their tiny flounce.

Questions spiral, they twist and twine,
Like a rollercoaster, oh how divine!
With each answer found, there's one more clue,
I giggle and shrug, what else is new?

## Whispers in the Void

I shouted loud into the void,
It echoed back, I was annoyed.
'Why's life so odd?' I dared to ask,
It whispered back, 'You're not up to the task!'

What's the sound of one hand clapping?
I'm confused, my thoughts are mapping.
Life quirked a brow, what a tease,
While I tried hard to catch the breeze.

Are fish as confused as I am?
Swimming in circles, oh what a scam!
I tossed a worm to make a friend,
But they swam off, what a trend!

In this cosmos, questions swirl,
Like my hair, all a tangled whirl.
With chuckles bright and joy so pure,
I ponder more, that's for sure!

## Unraveling the Unknown

I sat and thought of pizza pie,
Wondering how it could touch the sky.
The cheese said, 'Just stretch and believe!'
While the crust giggled, 'You'll never leave!'

Why do socks always lose their pair?
It's a mystery, ask without care.
They wander off, where could they go?
Maybe to a sock ballet show!

If time has hands, where do they meet?
In coffee shops or on the street?
I spilled my drink and watched it flow,
Time laughed at me, 'Just let it go!'

With questions dancing like fireflies,
In the night where the laughter lies.
Each riddle brings a grin or two,
In this funny quest, we wander through.

**Veils of Uncertainty**

In a world of might and maybe,
I search for signs, it's kinda crazy.
Why do socks always go missing?
While the universe keeps on twisting.

Do fish ever feel ocean's dread?
Or do they swim 'til they're well-fed?
Is grass greener on the other side?
Or just the place where sheep abide?

Why is chocolate never a sin?
If happiness is found within?
Do trees gossip about the breeze?
Or laugh at how we're on our knees?

Questions bounce like rubber balls,
In life's game, it's funny, y'all!
Yet somehow we'll play on, true,
Chasing thoughts like morning dew.

## Mirrors of the Mind

Gazing in mirrors, who do I see?
A puzzled face that looks back at me.
Do cats think they're all that keen?
Or just plotting to be the queen?

Why do we worry, what's the point?
When pizza's always our best joint?
Do clouds ever ponder their fate?
While they float about so great?

Why do we ask 'what's the deal'?
When laughter is more of a meal?
Is the moon just a giant lamp?
For night owls in a nighttime camp?

Oh, mind's a maze of tangled yarn,
Where questions sprout like fields of corn.
But just like socks—each pair is neat,
Life's full circle is bittersweet.

## Endless Whispers of Inquiry

Why do we cringe at awkward chats?
While pondering life's strange little facts?
Do holes in cheese hold mysteries?
Or just a cause for mockeries?

Does the rain bring out silly moods?
Or just wash away our brooding dudes?
Are we but ants on a grand scale?
Or just walking tales wrapped in a veil?

When do we know to just let go?
When the ice cream hits in full flow!
Do sneakers feel our every stride?
Or just carry us where we hide?

Life runs like an endless race,
With punchlines hidden in every place.
Every question a playful jest,
A whisper, a laugh—just let it rest!

## **Circles of Thought**

Round and round thoughts do spin,
Is it deeper wisdom or just din?
Why do plants chase the sunlight?
While we sit here, holding on tight?

Do fish swap tales in streams they roam?
Or just swim in their cozy home?
Why do we think the grass looks bold?
When really it's just our hearts that fold?

Can dogs see the ghosts we fear?
Or just bark at things that aren't here?
Why do we giggle at our own plight?
When the world's spinning with such delight?

In circles, questions never cease,
Life's a puzzle, a silly piece.
Let's dance in loops, and with a cheer,
Enjoying each question year by year!

## The Spectrum of Searching

In a quest for truth, I seek a clue,
A map to guide me, a fortune too.
Yet every answer leads to more,
Like a cat chasing its tail on the floor.

Do I want to know why the sky is blue?
Or what the world thinks of my best shoe?
Questions pile up like laundry, oh dear,
I just want to sip my cold root beer!

Where do socks vanish, where do they go?
Is there a portal, a sock-keeping show?
These mysteries tickle, they make me grin,
So many questions, where do I begin?

Life's a riddle, a jigsaw of jest,
With every odd query, I feel so blessed.
Let's keep asking while we dance and play,
In this zany maze, we'll find our way!

## **Elysian Dilemmas**

What's the best flavor of ice cream to try?
Mint chip? Chocolate? Or apple pie?
Decisions spin 'round like a merry-go-round,
While I weigh options, the world spins around.

Do I want pajamas or a dress to wear?
Will it rain today? I haven't a care.
Lost in choices, my head feels like fluff,
Is coffee better, or just plain old stuff?

Should I dance in the rain or stay inside?
Each dilemma causes a giggle, a slide.
Life spins in circles, a perplexing scene,
Should I just flip a coin, or keep it routine?

With laughter echoing through each silly quest,
I'll embrace all the questions, I'm truly blessed.
For in the confusion, I find such delight,
Elysian dilemmas make everything bright!

**The Compass of Doubt**

With a compass of confusion, I wander astray,
North looks like south on this wibbly way.
Am I lost or just on a fun little spree?
Every turn leads to more curiosity!

Should I take the shortcut through the park?
Or bypass the fountain that glows after dark?
Choices, oh choices, they tumble and sway,
Like my lunch that just spilled on the way!

Is it really that urgent? Should I even care?
Or should I sit down and eat my eclair?
Here in the maze of my mind's silly dance,
Every "what if" feels like a chance!

Life's compass spins wildly, yet I'm not in fright,
Each path, each question, brings giggles and light.
So I'll chuckle along on this whimsical route,
With a wink and a laugh, I'll flip every doubt!

## Fragments of Fascination

Why do we ponder the oddest of things?
Like why do the birds always practice their sings?
Is it for us, or is it a show?
Such fragments of thought, it's amusing, you know?

Do fishes ever wonder what's under the sea?
Or do they just swim and sip on their tea?
Questions flutter like bees in the air,
With every small riddle, I giggle and stare!

Should I wear mismatched socks on this date?
Or polish my shoes to feel truly great?
Life's little puzzles are tender and sweet,
Like a funny surprise in a bowl of treats!

So let's weave our questions into the night,
With smiles and laughter, everything feels right.
In this tapestry of quirk and delight,
Fragments are gems that sparkle so bright!

www.ingramcontent.com/pod-product-compliance
Lightning Source LLC
Chambersburg PA
CBHW051640160426
43209CB00004B/733